SPORTING SKILLS

SWIMMING

CLIVE GIFFORD

WAYLAND

First published in 2008 by Wayland

Wayland
Hachette Children's Books
338 Euston Road
London NW1 3BH

Wayland Australia
Level 17/207 Kent Street
Sydney, NSW 2000

Managing Editor: Rasha Elsaeed
Produced by Tall Tree Ltd
Editor: Jon Richards
Designer: Ben Ruocco
Photographer: Michael Wicks
Consultant: Helen Tattershall

British Library Cataloguing in Publication Data

Gifford, Clive
  Swimming. - (Sporting skills)
  1. Swimming - Juvenile literature
  I. Title
  797.2'1

ISBN 9780750253789

Printed in China

Wayland is a division of Hachette Children's
Books, an Hachette Livre UK company.

Picture credits
All photographs taken by Michael Wicks,
except;
Cover Dreamstime.com/Iris Schneider,
5 Eddy Lemaistre/For Picture/Corbis

Acknowledgements
The author and publisher would like to thank
the following people for their help and
participation in this book:
Krystina and Adelle Hall, Dilan and Dinay
Savani, Molly and Thomas Landolfi and
Ellie Dyke.

The website addresses (URLs) included in this
book were valid at the time of going to press.
However, because of the nature of the
Internet, it is possible that some addresses
may have changed, or sites may have changed
or closed down since publication. While the
author and Publisher regret any inconvenience
this may cause the readers, no responsibility
for any such changes can be accepted by
either the author or the Publisher.

Disclaimer
In preparation of this book, all due care has
been exercised with regard to the advice,
activities and techniques depicted. The
publishers regret that they can accept no
liability for any loss or injury sustained.
When learning a new sport it is important
to get expert tuition and to follow a
manufacturer's instructions.

CONTENTS

WHAT IS SWIMMING?

Swimming is a water sport that is one of the most popular leisure pursuits in the world, carried out in lakes, rivers and seas as well as indoor and outdoor pools. It is one of the best forms of exercise as it builds endurance levels, muscle strength and heart and lung fitness. Many athletes in other sports use swimming as an important part of their training. Hundreds of thousands of swimmers take part in swimming races and competitions held for all levels and age groups.

IN COMPETITION

Swimming is one of just a handful of sports that have been present at every Summer Olympics since the first modern games in 1896. Top competitions today are organised by national swimming associations and FINA, the *Fédération Internationale de Natation*, which runs swimming competitions around the world. Competitions are held for backstroke, breaststroke, butterfly and freestyle strokes. In freestyle competitions, any stroke can be used, although swimmers tend to use the front crawl as it is the fastest stroke. Races for each stroke are held over a large range of distances from 50-metre (167-feet) sprints to endurance races measured in kilometres.

The pool

Competition pools come in two main sizes. Short-course events are held in 25-metre-long (83-feet-long) pools, while long-course events are held in 50-metre-long (167-feet-long) pools. The pools are divided into at least eight lanes that are about 2.5 metres (8.5 feet) wide. Officials start the race, check times and make sure that swimmers perform the strokes correctly and make the correct turns at the ends of the pool.

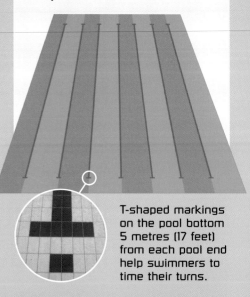

T-shaped markings on the pool bottom 5 metres (17 feet) from each pool end help swimmers to time their turns.

Two competing swimmers dive in as their team-mates complete their legs of a relay race (see pages 28–29).

Lanes in a swimming pool are separated by plastic floats strung on a cable stretched along the pool.

Many races end in close finishes. Winners are often those swimmers who best time their surge and touch of the end wall. In top competitions where fractions of a second can separate the swimmers, touch pads are fitted to the end of each lane. These are connected to automatic computers to ensure accurate race times.

DEDICATION

To be a top swimmer requires great dedication and sacrifice. Thousands of hours must be spent in training to develop the fitness, skill and speed to compete at a high level. A top swimmer like America's multi-Olympic medallist Michael Phelps will swim as much as 80,000 metres (267,000 feet) per week during the endurance-building part of his training. This distance will drop to around 50,000–60,000 metres (166,667–200,000 feet) as swimmers concentrate on improving their speed, and spend just 10–15 per cent of this swimming time at full racing speed.

Australian swimmer Ian Thorpe (right) celebrates after winning the 200 metre freestyle race at the 2004 Olympic Games in Athens, Greece.

TRAINING AND EQUIPMENT

Competitive swimming places huge demands on all parts of a competitor's body. Swimmers are taught to warm-up and stretch, to train hard, working on different aspects of their fitness and technique, and to follow their coach's instructions and drills carefully.

Stretching

Swimming uses most of the body's muscles, so these need to be fully warmed-up and stretched before and after a swimmer takes part in training or a competitive race. Warming up through moderate levels of swimming or jogging out of the pool gets the blood pumping around the body. All the main muscle groups of the body, especially those in the shoulders, arms, back and legs are then stretched. Ask your coach or swimming instructor to show you a thorough stretching programme.

Swimmers perform a shoulder muscle stretch called a posterior handclasp stretch. With the handclasp stretch, you should try to stretch your hands so that they touch each other behind your back. Then swap the arm positions around and repeat the stretch.

Two young swimmers wear swimsuits, caps and goggles. Good female swimming costumes are cut high around the neck and are usually made of stretchy material to fit closely. Male competitive swimmers either wear small trunks or closely fitting all-in-one bodysuits. Shorts are more popular for leisure swimming.

TRAIN TO GAIN

The amount of training depends on a swimmer's age, ability level and the access to local pools. Younger swimmers should concentrate on improving their swimming technique. At older ages and higher levels, training is split up into the five S's – skill, stamina, strength, speed and suppleness. Stamina is the ability to perform work for long periods. This and strength are mainly increased through long endurance training sessions in the pool.

A coach takes two swimmers through the hand and arm movements of the front crawl by the poolside. Swimmers should work closely with their coaches to improve and refine their swimming techniques.

KITTED OUT

Get your coach to advise you on suitable swimsuits and good-quality goggles. Your swimsuit should be comfortable and not contain inside seams as these may rub and cause discomfort after long periods of swimming. While your swimming costume should be close fitting, your tracksuit, which is important for staying warm when out of the water, should be loose and comfortable.

This swimmer (left) is adjusting the fit of his goggles, making sure that they sit comfortably over his eyes and form a seal on his face to stop water from seeping in.

A swimmer with long hair tucks it underneath a swimcap which also covers the ears. This helps the swimmer to be more streamlined in the water, as well as stopping her hair from getting in her face.

FAST STARTS

Swimmers need a fast start to give them an early advantage in a race. The grab dive is used for breaststroke, butterfly and front crawl, while backstroke has its own starting technique.

STARTING PROCEDURE

Breaststroke, front crawl and butterfly swimmers start their races on top of a starting block – a large block fitted to one end of the pool. A single long blast of the referee's whistle tells swimmers to stand on top of the block or enter the water if it is a backstroke race. The referee then hands over to the starter who asks the swimmers to 'take their marks'. The swimmers move to the front of the blocks and get into the starting position. The starter begins the race with a gunshot, whistle or a shout of 'go!'.

DID YOU KNOW?

In major competitions, a false-start rope is held 15 metres (50 feet) down the pool from the start of a race. If there is a false start, the rope is dropped to alert swimmers that the race has been stopped.

Grab dive

1 This swimmer has got into the starting position. Her toes and hands grip the block, her knees are slightly bent and she is looking at the water just in front of the block.

2 The swimmer reacts to the start signal by pulling on the block to move her body forwards and down. The knees bend further and the arms start to swing forwards.

3 The legs drive off the blocks powerfully to send the swimmer both upwards and outwards. The arms extend upwards and forwards to bring the hands close together and with the fingers pointing towards the water.

4 The swimmer lifts her hips to raise her legs up with her feet pointing back. The hands slice a hole in the surface and the back arches as the body follows into the water.

As the swimmer enters the water, she makes herself as streamlined as possible. See how her hands are stretched forward and her feet are pointed back.

GLIDE AND DRAG

The dive or backstroke start are both designed to power the swimmer away. Once in the water, the swimmer's aim is to lose as little speed as possible. Drag is the resistance a swimmer encounters as he or she moves through the water. Keeping the body as streamlined as possible reduces the amount of drag.

Back crawl

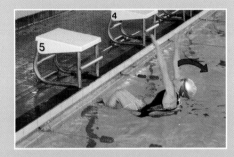

1 At the 'take your marks' signal, the swimmer holds the rail fitted to the front of the starting block. She pulls herself into a coiled up position with her head tucked down and her elbows flexed. Her feet are either level or staggered, but both must stay underwater throughout the start.

2 As the race starts, the swimmer pulls up with her arms, releases her hold and pushes hard with her feet away from the wall. Her body and the tops of her legs rise out of the water. She tilts her head back, throws her arms backwards and arches her body.

3 With the hands together and the head between the arms, the hands enter the water followed by the rest of the body. The back straightens on entry and the fingers point towards the surface. The swimmer then surfaces to start her first stroke.

False Starts

With races won by fractions of seconds, swimmers know that a good, fast start is essential. However, while they want to react as quickly to the start signal as possible, they do not want to commit a false start. Swimmers must stay perfectly still on their blocks before the race starts. If they do not or if they leave their blocks before the start signal is given, then they have committed a false start. While some junior swimming galas allow a swimmer to make one or more false starts, the rules at the highest level are strict. A swimmer making a false start is disqualified from the race.

FRONT CRAWL

Swimming well is all about maximising propulsion and minimising drag. The front crawl has one arm travelling overhead and entering the water and pulling back before the other arm performs the same movement. These movements generate a lot of propulsion and the least drag, making the front crawl the fastest of all the strokes.

FLAT AND SHALLOW

The front crawl requires a swimmer's body to be almost flat and as streamlined as possible. The hips should be just below the surface of the water with the shoulders effectively 'resting' on the surface. The face is underwater with the waterline on the forehead and the eyes looking about an arm's length ahead.

The catch point is where the hand fixes in the water, while the swimmer pulls the body past the hand.

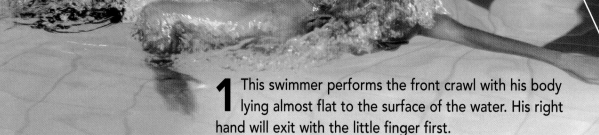

1 This swimmer performs the front crawl with his body lying almost flat to the surface of the water. His right hand will exit with the little finger first.

2 The right elbow is kept high and the hand leaves the water with the palm facing away from the thigh as it swings forward.

3 The left hand passes close to the body as the right arm reaches past the head and spears the water ahead of the swimmer.

Side view

4 The right arm extends to full reach, sweeps out to shoulder width and 'catches' the water (see above).

1 **Stretch.** After entering the water as smoothly as possible, the arm reaches forwards until it is at full stretch.

2 **Downsweep.** The arm and hand sweep downwards and outwards with the elbow still kept high.

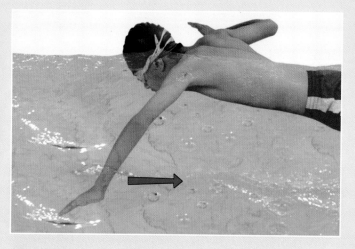

3 **Insweep.** The angle of the hand, or its pitch, changes as the arm swings backwards and in towards the centre of the body.

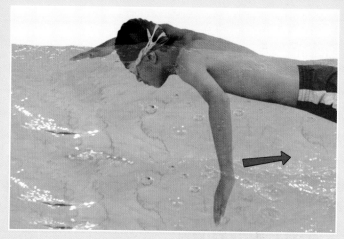

4 **Upsweep.** When close to the centre of the body, the hand changes pitch and accelerates through to the thigh.

STREAMLINING AND RHYTHM

You need to stay as streamlined as possible throughout the stroke in order to cut through the water. During the stroke, the arms need to follow a narrow path as the swimmer pulls his or her body through the water in order to help with the streamlining of the entire body.

5 **Recovery.** The hand exits the water with the little finger first. For its recovery phase, the arm is relaxed and the elbow held high.

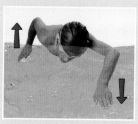

Viewed from the front, you can see how narrow the arm cycle is using front crawl (compare this with breaststroke or butterfly).

11

MORE FRONT CRAWL

The front crawl relies on smooth and continuous movements of both the arms and the legs. As one arm starts a new stroke, the other arm completes its stroke. All the time, the legs kick smoothly and strongly to aid balance and to give some additional force to move you forwards.

FRONT CRAWL KICK

Kicking the legs helps to keep the body balanced and centered so that the arms can generate most of the forward force. The front crawl kick involves an alternating and continuous up-and-down movement of the legs. The whole leg is used during the kick, starting at the thigh, and not just the part below the knee. Swimmers usually complete four or six leg kicks for every complete arm cycle.

S-PULL PATTERN

The arm stroke sees the hand follow an S-shaped path or S-pull in the water for each stroke. This 'sculling' motion of the hand enables the hand to be fixed in the water, while the swimmer pulls the body past the hand.

After entry, the swimmer's hand turns slightly to 'catch' the water.

As the arm is pulled down, so the hand is first moved outwards.

About halfway through the stroke, the hand is twisted and brought back in.

BREATHING IN

Breathing is performed to the side with as little disruption to the stroke as possible. As one arm enters the water, the swimmer's shoulders roll down towards that arm. The head, which normally lies in the water, turns to the opposite side so that the mouth can open and take a breath in.

This swimmer turns his head smoothly in order to breathe. The right side of his face still remains in the water.

Breathing Out

There are two ways of breathing out when swimming. Explosive breathing is where a swimmer forces the air out of the lungs sharply just before taking in a new breath. Trickle breathing is where the swimmer lets the air out of the lungs gradually throughout the arm cycle. This has to be timed so that the breath has all but gone as the head is turned out of the water to breathe in.

COMMON FAULTS

There are a number of common faults that inexperienced swimmers make with front crawl. One common mistake is to generate a lot of splashing with the hands and with the feet. White water should be avoided as much as possible, with the hands spearing the water cleanly and the kick starting below the water's surface.

This swimmer's arm is travelling too high and it is almost vertical during the recovery phase. This wastes energy and can slow you down.

This swimmer is lifting the whole of her head up and out of the water to breathe. This movement will slow her down, create a lot of unnecessary drag and force her lower body down.

This swimmer has bent her leg far too much at the knee so that her kicking action takes her foot completely out of the water. This loses power and makes the swimmer unbalanced in the water. The kicking action should involve the whole leg, with the foot only ever rising as high as the surface.

BREASTSTROKE

Breaststroke is believed to be the oldest of the four main swimming strokes. It is the only stroke where your arms and legs stay under the water for the entire time. As a result, it is the slowest of the four strokes.

BODY POSITION

Breaststroke is a popular beginner's stroke because it can be swum with the head and face always out of the water. For faster breaststroke swimming, the face is placed in the water to the forehead during the glide phase. The head rises up and out with the shoulders to breathe, as the arm action and subsequent kick are performed. The basic body position is not as flat as all the other stokes, as the body slopes down to the hips so that the feet remain underwater.

1 This breaststroke swimmer performs the glide forward, keeping in a streamlined position. Her face is down in the water and she is looking slightly forwards. Her arms are stretched out and pressed against her ears.

Side view

2 The hands and arms begin to sweep outwards. The palms of the hands are turned out, the fingers point down and the hands are at the catch point (see page 10).

3 With the elbows staying high, the arms and hands sweep out, down and back firmly. As the hands travel under the elbows, the palms turn inwards.

4 The elbows follow the hands forwards along the centre line of the body to the chin. The arms stretch forwards to glide smoothly, with the hands close together.

This swimmer's head rises to breathe just prior to performing the leg kick, following which she will glide.

ARMS AND LEGS

In simple terms, the arms move in a small circle under the water. They start stretched out in front of you, before they make a small circle to underneath your chin with the palms pressed together. Then, they stretch forward again to complete one arm cycle. The feet are drawn up towards the bottom, the knees are hip-width apart and the toes turn outwards and upwards to kick in a backwards, circular motion with your heels coming together.

WARM-UP

Breaststroke can put pressure on the lower back and cause knee strain, so it should not be performed at all until a swimmer has fully warmed up.

Breathing

Breathing when performing breaststroke is simple as the shoulders rise naturally when your arms complete their sweep and are coming in underneath your body.

Breathing out can be performed as your head re-enters the water. Try to time your breathing so that you do not lurch your head up too early to gasp for air, as this will slow you down.

This front-on shot of a swimmer performing the breaststroke highlights the symmetry of the arm and leg movements. The shoulders, hips and knees must be on the same horizontal plane throughout the stroke, otherwise a swimmer will lose his or her balance in the water, resulting in a slower speed.

MORE BREASTSTROKE

The breaststroke involves two sets of relatively complex actions – one for the arms and one for the legs. These movements can be practised separately, using floats or a woggle to support the arms or legs. It is also a good idea to first practise the breaststroke leg kick on your back before attempting it on your front.

Leg action

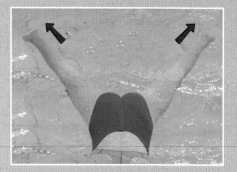

1 During the glide stage, the legs are extended behind the swimmer with toes pointing back.

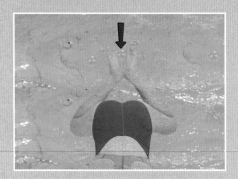

2 The knees bend and the heels are brought up towards the swimmer's bottom with the soles pointing upwards. The knees part to hip width. This is the leg recovery stage.

3 Just before the kick begins, the feet are turned outwards in what is called a dorsi-flexed position. The kick is backwards in a circular motion. It is the first part of the kick that provides the main propulsive force.

4 The leg kick accelerates backwards and downwards until the legs are fully extended.

WEDGE AND WHIP KICKS

Beginners and casual swimmers often use a kicking style called the wedge kick. This involves the swimmer kicking his or her feet out wide during the kick. The whip kick is a narrower, faster kick that is normally used by competitive swimmers. The main thrust of the whip kick is made by the lower legs and insides of the feet as they drive back in a curved, whip-like action, outside the line of the knees.

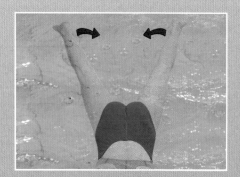

5 The legs begin to sweep back together and the toes are pointed to end up in the stretched, streamlined position shown in the first stage, known as the glide.

16

1 From this front-on view, you can see how streamlined the swimmer is during the glide stage of the breaststroke. Her arms are stretched with her fingers pointing straight ahead.

2 With the palms of the hands pitched outwards, the swimmer sweeps outwards and slightly downwards until her arms reach the catch position.

3 From the catch position, the swimmer sweeps her hands briefly downwards and slightly outwards, with the elbows bent and kept high.

TIMING AND SYMMETRY

Swimming the breaststroke well requires very good timing. A common mistake for beginners is to start the leg kick back at the same time as the arms pull and sweep back. Think 'pull-kick-glide', with your feet beginning their kick out and back as the arms push forwards from the chin to glide

COMMON FAULTS

A number of faults can occur during breaststroke. Legs should stay underwater at all times. Screw-kicking can occur when one hip or knee is lower than the other or when one foot is turned out correctly and the other is turned in, or turned out but with the toes pointing downwards rather than up towards the knees.

4 Before the hands get to shoulder level, the palms pitch inwards. The elbows follow the hands towards the centre line of the swimmer's body.

Swimmers practise their breaststroke in a pool training session. The stroke requires excellent timing between the different movements of the arms and legs.

5 The arms will then stretch forwards for the gliding stage.

BACK CRAWL

Back crawl is the only stroke where competitors start in the water. It has some similarities in movement and streamlining to the front crawl, particularly its leg kick.

BASIC MOVEMENT

The back crawl involves a continuous alternating movement of the arms and legs. The leg kick is an alternate up and down action started from the hip, with the legs passing close together. As one arm pulls through the water strongly, the other arm recovers out of the water, led by the thumb and, remaining straight, reaches behind the swimmer's head to re-enter the water with the little finger entering first.

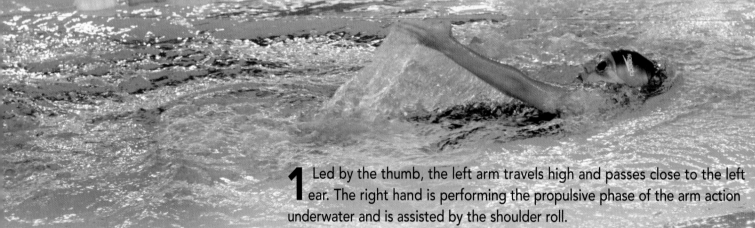

1 Led by the thumb, the left arm travels high and passes close to the left ear. The right hand is performing the propulsive phase of the arm action underwater and is assisted by the shoulder roll.

Side view

2 The right hand pushes the water away as it heads close to the swimmer's thigh. The left arm slides into the water; elbow, then forearm, and finally the hand.

3 As the left arm enters the water, the right hand is stretched down and outwards to catch the water. The shoulders start to roll to the right.

4 The left arm makes its pulling stroke through the water with the shoulders rolled to the left. The right arm has risen up and is recovering through the air.

HEAD AND BODY POSITION

The basic body position sees the backstroke swimmer lying horizontally on his or her back. The swimmer's head is still, with the eyes looking upwards and backwards, requiring the chin to tuck in a little. By keeping the hips high at or just under the surface, the legs lie slightly lower than the body. The legs are straight with the toes pointed. The body rolls along its length. The head leads the stroke and keeping it still helps to keep you as streamlined as possible.

As this swimmer's left arm recovers, it travels vertically through the air, fully extended and brushes past her left ear. This helps her to position the correct streamlined entry of the arm back into the water.

This back crawl swimmer (below) shows an excellent head and body position. The head is still, the eyes look up and slightly backwards.

Flagged rope

This line fitted with flags is suspended across the pool 5 metres (17 feet) from the end. It offers a visual sign to backstroke swimmers that the pool wall is approaching. Back crawl swimmers get used to judging distances by also counting the number of strokes they have made and by noting places on the pool ceiling.

BREATHING

With your face out of the water all of the time, breathing is easy but should be regular. A breath should be taken with every stroke cycle, normally inhaling as one arm recovers and breathing out as the other arm recovers. An alternative is to breathe in and out regularly as the arms recover through the air.

MORE BACK CRAWL

As back crawl is performed on the back, the amount of power that can be exerted by the arms is limited. Therefore, a good back stroke needs a strong leg kick and has a shoulder roll technique which helps the swimmer to get a better catch in the water.

Leg kick

1 This swimmer's legs are extended with the feet stretched at the ankles. The right leg remains straight for most of the downwards movement.

2 The right leg is then kicked from the hip with a strong fluid motion. The knee stays underwater, but the feet should just break the surface, while the ankles are kept flexible.

LEG KICKS

Constant, even leg kicking helps stop the swimmer from snaking back and forth across the lane and losing valuable time and rhythm. The leg kick is alternate and continuous throughout the stroke and a little deeper than in the front crawl. The legs must drive down and up to equal distances and with the same amount of force. A good backstroker will complete six kicks to one arm cycle. Long-distance or recreational swimmers may only complete two or four leg kicks for each arm cycle.

To make as big a paddle as possible while kicking, you should turn your feet inwards. This is called intoeing.

The crucial back crawl arm action can be worked on in training without using the legs. This swimmer is using a pool buoy gripped between his upper thighs. This training aid helps place you in a good body position with the hips high so that you can work on your arm stroke.

1 The swimmer's right arm recovers through the air with the hand rotating at the wrist so that the palm is facing outwards.

2 The right arm enters the water, little finger first, with the hand making as little splash as possible. The hand sweeps down and outwards to catch the water.

3 From the catch, the elbow bends at right angles and the pitch of the hand changes to sweep inwards.

THE S-PULL

Some beginners are taught to use a straight arm action in the water with the arm sweeping back towards the swimmer's body, but this is not as efficient or fast as the S-pull method. The S-pull sees the arm enter the water and then sweep in a S-shaped pattern under the water. The arm is bent at the elbow and then finally straightens as it gets close to the thigh.

COMMON FAULTS

A common mistake is to 'sit' in the water with the bottom dropped so that the hips are not near the surface and the legs are too low. Other common faults include the legs being too far apart and the arms not entering the water shoulder-width apart.

4 The right hand accelerates as the fingers point sideways and the hand pitch changes so that the palm faces down. The sweep ends with a hard downward push to below the thigh.

While the head keeps straight and flat, the body rolls from the shoulder to the same side as the arm which is pulling in the water. This helps the arm to pull the water from a deep, strong position.

5 The right arm will exit thumb first. The hand and arm start to rise and will shortly leave the water. The left arm is relaxed and straight as it recovers over the water.

BUTTERFLY

The butterfly is the second-fastest stroke, but it is physically the most demanding to perform. It sees a swimmer surge forwards and out of the water in a spectacular and powerful movement.

BODY POSITION AND MOVEMENT

Viewed from a distance, the butterfly stroke looks as if the swimmer plunges deep into the water and then surges high out of it. The stroke relies on a wave-like movement of the swimmer's body. However, the head should never rise too high or sink too low in the water. Both shoulders should always be level with each other, and the head leads the rest of the body throughout the stroke.

1 The head and shoulders surge out of the water as the swimmer takes a good breath. The arms leave the water elbows first and the hips rise almost to the surface.

Side view

2 The swimmer's head leads the body back into the water and the arms swing wide past the head. The arms are kept low and almost straight over the water as the hips begin to rise for the kick.

3 The arms enter the water about shoulder-width apart and ahead of the swimmer. The thumbs enter first as the hands half-pitch out. The arms are bent, with the elbows higher than the hands.

4 As the hands sweep outwards and downwards, the hips drop. Then the hips start to rise as the hands sweep in and then accelerate upwards through to the thighs.

THE DOLPHIN KICK

The kick used in the butterfly is different from the front crawl kick or the breaststroke whip kick. Unlike the front crawl kick, the two legs move together throughout the wave-like movement up and down. This is called the dolphin kick.

The movement should start from the hips. The legs stay close together, with the ankles relaxed and the toes pointed. The kick requires the knees to bend to almost right angles – far more than the front or back crawl. The leg kick generates only a little propulsion, but it helps the swimmer to maintain a horizontal body position and it also balances the arm action.

An important part of the butterfly stroke is the rise of the head out of the water before the arms leave the water. Here, the swimmer's head is up as she takes a breath. The arms now rise out of the water and the head starts to dip down back down.

Leg kick

1 With the feet just breaking the surface, the toes are pointed and the legs bent at the knees. The upper legs begin driving down from the hips.

2 The lower legs start their whip-like action downwards with the feet together. They generate much of the power of the kick in their downwards movement.

3 The legs kick down until they are fully extended.

4 The swimmer remains horizontal for a short period during the glide, before the legs start to rise, again led by the hips.

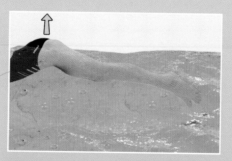

5 The swimmer's bottom lifts out of the water with the hips bent so that the legs remain below the water line. The legs are now ready to start the next kick sequence.

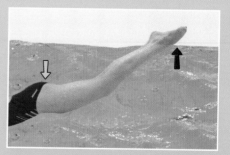

6 The upper legs are pushed down and the toes rise just out of the water. The tops of the feet then press backwards and downwards to drive below the surface again.

MORE BUTTERFLY

There is a lot to practise with the butterfly, particularly the arm stroke which recovers over the water and then sweeps in a keyhole or hourglass shape under the water. The stroke also relies on excellent timing between the swimmer's head, arms, body and legs.

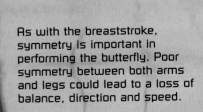

TIMING AND BREATHING

Timing is crucial with the butterfly. Both arms and legs have to move at the same time as each other. There are two kicks per arm cycle. The first kick (the minor) occurs as the hands enter the water and sweep past. The second kick (the major) is stronger as it has to kick the swimmer out of the water to enable the recovery of the arms. Breathing out takes place as the head rises just before the arms start their recovery stroke. The swimmer breathes in when the face is clear of the water. Many swimmers choose only to breathe every other arm stroke.

COMMON FAULTS

Until the swimmer is able to move through the water with a wave-like motion, without using the arms, he or she will have great difficulty performing the correct leg and arm actions. You should work hard with a coach to perfect the wave-like body movement before even attempting the arm action.

As with the breaststroke, symmetry is important in performing the butterfly. Poor symmetry between both arms and legs could lead to a loss of balance, direction and speed.

Butterfly training

Butterfly may feel clumsy and awkward at first, but the movements will become easier the more you practise. Swimmers need to have a good undulating body and leg action before attempting the whole stroke. The butterfly stroke can be tiring and coaches often advise beginners to train and practise in short bursts.

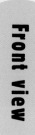

Front view

1 The hands enter the water about shoulder-width apart. The palms face half outwards and the arms extend to full stretch.

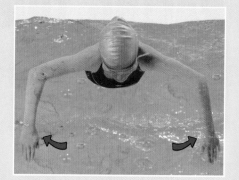

2 The hands then sweep slightly outwards and downwards to catch the water. From the catch, there is a short downsweep. The elbows bend and remain higher than the hands.

3 The hands start to sweep and rotate inwards, pressing the water back as they move towards the centre-line of the body.

4 The hands now sweep outwards again and the elbows straighten.

5 The arms leave the water, with the little fingers uppermost.

6 The arms recover just above the water in a wide flinging movement. They stay low as they move over the water so that as little energy as possible is wasted.

7 As the arms pass shoulder level, they start to come inwards ready to slide into the water in front of the swimmer's shoulders to begin another stroke.

RACING TURNS

Many races are held over more than one length of the pool. Vital fractions of a second can be gained or lost when performing a turn. This is why swimmers work so hard on their racing turns, making them as quick and as smooth as possible.

TIMING TURNS

Turns are often split into four phases – the approach to the pool wall, the actual touch and turn movements, the push off at the start of the new length of the pool, and the transition from pushing off to swimming the stroke. Many swimmers use the tee markings on the pool bottom (see page 4) as a guide to judging distances and timing their movements.

Front crawl

1 This swimmer approaches the wall at normal swimming speed.

2 The swimmer drops her chin to her chest as the last overarm recovery is completing.

3 The body bends at the hips and the head is forced down as the leading arm pulls to the hips on the final approach.

4 The body starts to tuck and both hands start to press downwards to help the swimmer rotate fully.

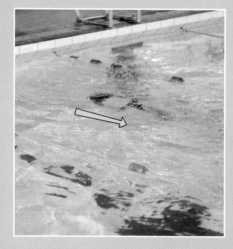

5 The swimmer plants her feet firmly on the pool wall and, still virtually on her back, she pushes off with knees bent to right angles, and with plenty of power. Both legs and arms extend to a streamlined position during the push-off phase as the swimmer rotates onto her front ready to start her first stroke.

Back turns

The most efficient backstroke turn permitted in competition sees the swimmer approach the wall on the back. As pictured here, on the last full backstroke, the swimmer crosses her recovering arm over her body so that it enters in line with the opposite shoulder. This helps the swimmer to roll onto her front. The turn is then completed as with the front crawl turn. At the push-off stage, the feet should be planted firmly on the wall. As the swimmer pushes against the wall, the arms and legs extend to a streamlined position.

TURN APPROACH

Try not to slow down on approaching the pool wall, as you need some speed in order to make the turn. In situations where you are a little short of the pool wall, an extra-hard kick rather than another full stroke can bring you closer. Turns require a lot of practice and the help of your swimming coach. Some swimmers practise turns by swimming widths of a pool rather than lengths.

Breaststroke

1 This swimmer is about to perform a turn for either breaststroke or butterfly. Approaching the wall at normal speed, it is essential that the swimmer touches the wall with both hands simultaneously. The arms should be fully extended at the point of touch.

2 As the touch is made, the knees bend and the hips continue to move towards the wall, causing the elbows to bend.

3 One hand is released from the wall as the knees and feet draw up under the body. The head turns to follow the leading hand, which is now thrown over the water to lead a streamlined path for the body to follow. The feet are planted firmly on the wall with the toes pointing downwards and sideways. The swimmer pushes off with a powerful thrust, extending her arms and legs to achieve a streamlined position ready to begin the transition to stroke.

RELAYS AND MEDLEYS

Relays involve teams of swimmers taking it in turns to perform the same stroke. Medleys feature swimmers performing all four major strokes in sequence and can involve individual swimmers or relay teams.

RELAYS

Relays are exciting races usually for four swimmers in a team. Each team member swims one or more lengths before 'handing over' to a team-mate. The next swimmer in a relay cannot leave the blocks or pool end until the previous team member has touched the wall. Judges are on hand to spot any breaking of this rule, which will result in a team being disqualified.

1 The swing start is the main form of start used in relay swimming. Unlike a normal race start, swimmers are allowed to move their arms, providing their feet are still on the blocks.

2 As the swimmer's team-mate touches the wall, she swings her arms forwards strongly, bends her legs to right angles, leans her body forwards and uses her legs to drive off the starting block powerfully.

3 The arms come forwards and together around and beyond the head as the push off from the starting block is complete. The legs thrust upwards and outwards.

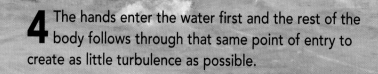

4 The hands enter the water first and the rest of the body follows through that same point of entry to create as little turbulence as possible.

28

TEAM MEDLEY

Medleys can be swum as a four swimmer relay with each swimmer performing one stroke. The relay begins with backstroke before moving on to breaststroke, butterfly and, finally, front crawl. Just like regular relay racing, one swimmer has to touch the wall before another can leave the blocks.

INDIVIDUAL MEDLEY

An individual medley event sees one swimmer swim all four major strokes in the following order – butterfly, backstroke, breaststroke and then front crawl.

A relay swimmer reaches for the pool wall. Precious fractions of a second can be lost if the swimmer misjudges the distance or timing of this touch.

Transitions

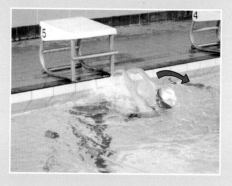

1 Medley races have rules regarding the transitions between the four strokes. Here, a swimmer comes to the end of their butterfly leg of the race and must change to backstroke.

2 As she touches the wall with both hands, she pulls her knees up underneath her body.

3 She rolls onto her back and pushes off with both legs. She finally extends her arms in front of her with the hands together as she uses the dolphin kick to move underwater before surfacing.

Making the transition from backstroke to breaststroke in an individual medley involves the swimmer first touching the wall with her hand while on her back. She then performs a backward roll, flipping her legs over so that her feet are close to the pool wall. She can then push off before starting her breaststroke.

GLOSSARY AND RESOURCES

Glossary

backstroke A stroke performed face up in the water, with the arms pulled high past the head and through the water and the legs kicking up and down.

blocks The starting platforms located behind each lane used for swimmers to enter the water. Blocks come in different designs and can be permanent or removable.

breaststroke A stroke performed face down in the water with the arms pulling through the water in a circular motion and the legs kicking with a pushing action.

butterfly A stroke performed face down in the water where the body performs a wave-like movement and the arms are brought over the head at the same time.

disqualification When a swimmer is taken out of a race and his or her performance not counted because a rule has been broken.

drag The resistance a swimmer's body encounters in the water when moving through it. Drag can slow you down.

explosive breathing Breathing out sharply just before taking a new breath.

false start A start in which one or more swimmers leaves the blocks before the starting signal.

front crawl A stroke performed face down in the water where the arms are brought over the head one at a time and the legs kick up and down.

Freestyle A competition in which swimmers can swim using a stroke style of their own choice.

heat An early race in an event which qualifies the fastest finishers for the semi-finals or final.

lane A narrow channel marked out with floating lines inside which a competitor must stay as they swim.

long course Events at swim meets, such as the Olympics, which use a 50-metre-long (167-feet-long) pool.

medley A combination event in which an individual swimmer or a relay team swim separate legs of backstroke, breaststroke, butterfly and freestyle.

recovery The part of your stroke where your arms or legs do not exert any force on the water. It usually means the part of the stroke that gets your arms or legs back to the stroke start.

resistance How water acts against your body and slows you down.

short course Events found at some swim meetings which use a 25-metre-long (83-feet-long) pool.

streamline The position used to gain maximum distance during a start and push-off from the wall in which the swimmer's body is as tight as it can be.

stroke cycle One complete arm and leg action of a swimming stroke.

trickle breathing Breathing gently out through the nose and mouth underwater between breaths.

tumble turn An underwater roll at the end of a length, used in some strokes to turn and push off with the feet.

Diet and nutrition

What you eat and drink daily and in the hours before training or a swim meet can affect your swimming performance. Try to eat a major meal about two-and-a-half to three hours before competition to give your body a chance to start digesting your food and getting energy from it. Lighter, easily-digested foods such as fruit, rice cakes, oatmeal cookies and plain muesli bars can be eaten as a small snack during a long swim meet. All the effort in training or competition and long periods spent in warm indoor pool areas in and out of the water can leave you short of fluids in your body. You should top up regularly with small amounts of water and occasionally juice or flat squash, not fizzy drinks.

As a swimmer you should be eating a healthy balanced diet every day to suit the amount of training you wish to do. Keep your intake of fast foods with high levels of fat or sugar down to a minimum. Instead, concentrate on eating foods full of protein and complex carbohydrates such as rice, pasta, fruit and vegetables, tuna and lean meats. Ask your coach for guidance on what you should eat.

swimming.about.com/
Head to the nutrition section shown on the left hand side and enjoy a series of useful articles and features on diet, nutrition and swimming.

www.swim.shetland.co.uk/Information/ SwimEats1.htm
A really useful article on diet and nutrition for young swimmers in two helpful parts.

www.mypyramid.gov/kids/index.html
Healthy eating is sometimes shown as a food pyramid. This website from the US Department of Agriculture provides lots of downloadable files and posters.

Resources

www.swimmingworldmagazine.com/technique/
The techniques webpages of *Swimming World* magazine are full of handy tips to improve your strokes.

www.dunedinswimteam.co.uk/swimming_tips.htm
A simple webpage with links to useful animations of the four main swimming strokes as well as photographs of the strokes in action.

news.bbc.co.uk/sport1/hi/other_sports/ swimming/default.stm
The BBC Sport webpages that deal with swimming include latest tournament news, technique tips and some useful videos and animations showing various swimming strokes.

www.fina.org/
Homepage of FINA (the *Fédération Internationale de Natation*), the international body that runs world swimming. A great place to head also for the rules of competitive swimming.

www.britishswimming.org/
Home on the internet of the Amateur Swimming Association which runs many aspects of swimming in the UK and lists swimming clubs in your area.

www.usaswimming.org/
The official site of USA Swimming, the organisation which runs competitive swimming in the United States.

www.swimming.org.au/
The Swimming Australia website contains details and photos of swim meets, information on elite Australian swimmers and a large database of swimming clubs all over Australia.

INDEX